PRAISE FOR *JOYPOWERED®* |

In *JoyPowered® Networking*, JoDee and Christine capture stories and advice that give the reader hope and direction for positive networking that can lead to great outcomes. Reading their personal stories helps readers see that networking throughout our daily lives can add meaning and richness and JOY to our careers and personal lives.

—Vern Schellenger, CEO, Contacts Count

NETWORKING is an interesting word. How do you define it? If you consider the word literally, you can view it as working to ensnare yourself and others in a net. That definition is not only facetious; it is also negative.

JoyPowered® Networking provides valuable insights into networking the opposite way by recommending a positive attitude instead. Authors JoDee Curtis' and Christine Burrows' unique style makes you feel like you're networking with them as you read their book. Each chapter offers networking nuggets enhanced by relatable stories about how they used them.

—Linda Comerford, Owner, Comerford Consulting

JoyPowered® Networking provides guidance on which chances to take, which relationships are worth pursuing and how to make decisions about enriching your network. JoDee Curtis and Christine Burrows show you how they developed their networks and offer you a path to create your own. *JoyPowered® Networking* is a must-read book for anyone who wants to benefit from *JoyPowered®* connections.

-—Kara A.

Publishing support provided by
Ignite Press
5070 N. Sixth St. #189
Fresno, CA 93710
www.IgnitePress.us

ISBN: 979-8-9888859-0-0
ISBN: 979-8-9888859-1-7 (E-book)

For bulk purchases and for booking, contact:
JoDee Curtis
networking@getjoypowered.com
getjoypowered.com

Library of Congress Control Number: 2023912407

Cover design by Sabeeh ul Hassan
Edited by Emily Miller
Interior design by Eswari Kamireddy

FIRST EDITION

joy⚙powered®
NETWORKING

Real-Life Stories and Advice for Getting the Best from Your Connections

JoDee Curtis and Christine Burrows

CONTENTS

PREFACE

The intention of the JoyPowered® series is to help readers find joy wherever they are. Sometimes we have to look for it, prioritize it, and talk about it. Sometimes it comes more naturally. Finding that joy will help us excel at work, in our family, on a team, or as an organization.

If you want to learn about finding joy in other areas of your life, check out the other books in the JoyPowered® series:

- *JoyPowered®: Intentionally Creating an Inspired Workspace[1]*
- *The JoyPowered® Family[2]*
- *The JoyPowered® Team[3]*
- *The JoyPowered® Organization[4]*

Christine Burrows, my co-author, was the inspiration for this book. We have worked together in the last few years to create Powered by Purple Ink, a network of workforce consultants throughout the United States. Although we felt very comfortable networking prior to forming PbPI, the process of building the network took our knowledge and skills to a whole new level.

Both Christine and I are natural networkers. We enjoy networking. We seek out opportunities to network. We thrive on JoyPowered® networking.

We have lots of stories to tell, and we share them as ways to illustrate our learning. We didn't become successful businesswomen with extensive professional networks without a few lessons from the school of hard knocks. We hope our stories give you encouragement and confidence to persevere in your goal to build more meaningful and valuable professional connections.

CliftonStrengths®

As a core of the JoyPowered® series, we share our passion for the CliftonStrengths® philosophy. It is the power of understanding what you do best (your strengths) and how you can aim your strengths to achieve excellence. The CliftonStrengths® assessment is a quick, easy, inexpensive way to discover your strengths.[5]

To purchase and take the CliftonStrengths® assessment, scan this QR code.

If you've taken the assessment and need a refresher on what your strengths mean, scan this QR code to see short descriptions.

Your strengths are not about what you do. They are about what drives you when you are doing it. If you haven't taken the CliftonStrengths® assessment, thoughtfully and intentionally consider times when you performed at your highest level, achieved success, and felt energized. Identify what was driving you when that happened.

Although we refer to CliftonStrengths® many times in this book, we also address ways others have had intentional JoyPowered® networking experiences without a formal understanding of CliftonStrengths®.

Who Is This Book For?

This book is for those who want to master the art of networking – AND find joy while doing so.

Create Your Own Action Plan

If you want to take notes while you read, check out Appendices A and B. Each time you feel inspired by an idea or story in this book, jot your insights down on either the insight (Appendix A) or action-planning worksheet (Appendix B). Your notes will become the inspiration you need, from first step to long-term strategy, to begin your personalized JoyPowered® networking action plan.

INTRODUCTION

N etworking.
How do you feel about it?

Does it excite you? Stress you out? Inspire you? Intimidate you? Confuse you?

Regardless of how you answer this question, this book is for you. Our goal in writing this book is to provide our readers inspiration and tactics for forming meaningful connections through networking. We will share the lessons we have learned over the years about why, when, how, and with whom to invest your time and energy to network and connect. We are writing for the job seeker, the business developer, the solopreneur, the bureaucrat, the aspiring leader, the veteran executive, the HR director, the marketer, the curious, the bold, the timid, the introvert, and the extrovert.

Networking has served us both well in our lives. We have formed a variety of meaningful connections through networking, including business relationships, friendships, mentorships, and advisorships. This book is our path to share what we have learned, but also to provide you steps and actions to guide you through your own networking journey.

We have grown successful careers and businesses through networking, and we both firmly believe that forming connections with others is an essential part of life and business. If we don't create opportunities for these connections to blossom, we aren't responding to our vital need to connect, form bonds, help one another along personal and professional journeys, and ultimately make the world a better place.

The Kickball Field as a Networking Venue

We met on a kickball field when we were in our forties. Our sons were running cross country together, and we were on a team of moms competing in a women's kickball tournament at their school. Long before JoDee had conceived JoyPowered®, we were experiencing JoyPower that sunny October day in the high school parking lot!

Since then, we've become close friends who have served one another as mentors, confidants, referral sources, and now business partners. For several years, we had a standing lunch date during which we would discuss the challenges of business ownership and board leadership, offer support and counsel, and enjoy our friendship.

> To reap the greatest benefits of connection, we must be curious, open-minded, open-hearted, and persistent.

Had we not followed up from that first JoyPowered® encounter on the kickball field, we would not have the benefit of our substantive and valuable connection now. Based upon our own experiences and the learnings we've gleaned over the years, we believe that some of the best relationships start in non-traditional ways. To reap the greatest benefits of connection, we must be curious, open-minded, open-hearted, and persistent.

We hope this book inspires you and motivates to improve your networking skills and infuse JoyPower into your connections.

What Happens When You Don't Network Effectively?

We all know people who are afraid to network, think of it as work (it does have the word "work" in it), or regard it as superficial. We clearly disagree. We see the impact that NOT networking has had on many people in a variety of ways, including:

- lack of connections to turn to when they find themselves looking for a new position
- low knowledge of business and the wide variety of work and jobs in their industry and others
- poor performance in their current roles as a result of not fully understanding the vision of the organization and how their work fits into the greater picture of the organization's success
- no mentors in their lives to turn to for learning and career advice
- low confidence in their professional capabilities as a result of not leveraging the knowledge of others in their field

Benefits of Networking

On the flip side, those who practice and hone their networking skills reap many benefits. If our story of meeting one another and enjoying the many fruits of that connection isn't enough to inspire you to become a JoyPowered® networker, then maybe these benefits will do the trick.

Networking, in general, can:

- build your reputation
- build trust and support
- invite opportunity
- inspire creative thinking
- increase knowledge
- build self-confidence
- have positive health benefits

Whatever your reason for wanting to become a JoyPowered® networker, be assured that your work will be fruitful. You WILL reap many benefits – not the least of which will be getting to know more interesting people.

A Word About Bad Networking

You likely have experienced non-JoyPowered® networking with people who:

- drone on and do not listen
- brag about themselves
- write you off because you do not have a title that interests them
- are disengaged
- don't follow up on a commitment they make
- are selfish
- place quantity of connections over quality

These folks give networking a bad name. We want you to experience all the benefits of connection through great networking and be able to weed through the not-so-great networking that happens all around us.

JoyPowered® networking is for people who:

- want to develop real connections
- see business (and the world) as an opportunity to develop themselves
- are curious to learn more, meet more people, and hear different perspectives
- value individual stories
- regard differences in others highly
- seek to share their stories with others in the interest of growth for all
- understand their role in the growth of their business

This is JoyPowered® networking. We will show you how to do it. Come along.

1

NETWORKER, KNOW YOURSELF

Networkers come in all different styles. Just because we are extroverts and genuinely enjoy networking doesn't mean that every extrovert is a good networker or that introverts can't be outstanding at networking and forming relationships as well.

I bet you've encountered plenty of extroverts who take over a conversation and seem to have no regard for engaging or listening. You've probably also met some introverts who are great listeners and say little, but what they do say is interesting. Great networking isn't about being able to work a room. It's about being able to meet a single person and mutually benefit by learning from each other.

The first step in being a JoyPowered® networker is to know yourself and claim your personal strengths. In other words, don't try to be someone you're not, or you will always feel uncomfortable. Others will sense that discomfort. This can have a lasting impact on how you are perceived when others meet you, so knowing and being yourself is key to enjoying and being good at networking.

Name It and Claim It

We work together at Purple Ink, a full-service HR consulting firm with a mission to inspire JoyPowered® work. As a strengths-based organization, Purple Ink utilizes the CliftonStrengths® assessment and framework to better know ourselves and one another[5]. The premise of

CliftonStrengths® is that we all have unique strengths. If we are able to understand them and hone them, years of Gallup research proves that we will be happier in our lives and work.

As members of the Purple Ink team, we seek to understand our strengths well and utilize them in our work and personal lives. This helps us identify work that each of us is well-suited to perform, collaborate effectively as a team, and optimize the joy we feel in being part of the overall mission of our business. It's downright magical how CliftonStrengths® has positively impacted each member of our organization and contributed to the success of every aspect of our business.

When it comes to forming meaningful relationships, we are both naturally well-suited to be good networkers. Here are our top strengths and how we tap them to be JoyPowered® networkers.

Christine's strengths as defined by Gallup[7]:

1. **Woo:** People who are especially talented in the Woo theme love the challenge of meeting new people and winning them over. They derive satisfaction from breaking the ice and making a connection with another person.

2. **Communication:** People who are especially talented in the Communication theme generally find it easy to put their thoughts into words. They are often good conversationalists and presenters.

3. **Activator:** People who are especially talented in the Activator theme can make things happen by turning thoughts into action. They are often impatient.

4. **Connectedness:** People who are especially talented in the Connectedness theme have faith in the links between all things. They believe there are few coincidences and that almost every event has a reason.

5. **Positivity:** People who are especially talented in the Positivity theme have an enthusiasm that is contagious. They are upbeat and can get others excited about what they are going to do.

Having Woo as my top strength means that I do not struggle with new people. I thrive on meeting new people and have a natural enthusiasm about the connection. I inherently enjoy networking and learning about others.

However, just because I can woo someone doesn't mean others actually want to be wooed, so, thankfully, I also have Connectedness in my top five strengths. This helps me go beyond the surface when meeting new people to see the connections and potential purpose in our knowing one another.

Add this philosophical belief to my Communication strength, and I spend a lot of time listening, asking questions, and positing possibilities with new connections. Then add in some Positivity, and I find true joy in the new connection. It often feels brimming with unlimited potential.

Finally, my Activator is all about getting the party started. It can mean that if something great is going to happen with the relationship, it's going to start quickly. It can also bring with it an impatience that may need tempering.

For example, I served six years on the school board for the private high school my children attended. For the first two years, I was the vice chair, then the chair for three years, and finally served in an emeritus position for one year. Here's how my strengths came into play:

- **Positivity:** When I first joined the board, I spent time getting to know others and feeling my way into the organization. I supported the initiatives of the group and was deliberate in my efforts to bring a positive spirit of collaboration.
- **Woo:** As I became more comfortable in my role, I was able to tap my Woo strength to find and drive consensus. This became even more valuable as I moved into leadership, but it was an asset I developed from the start and was able to lean on when we needed to make tough decisions.
- **Communication:** Being a strong communicator was extremely

valuable during my time on the board. This was not just about articulating ideas, but also about listening to others and finding ways to facilitate discussion. When we conducted an annual strategic planning initiative, being able to facilitate, listen, summarize, and provide feedback were vital skills I was able to tap into.

Utilizing my strengths not only served me tremendously in performing my duties as a member and a leader, but also in forming strong and enduring relationships with many stakeholders in this community. I remember saying to myself when I first took over the chair position, "Don't try to be Joe (my predecessor). Be yourself." It was incredibly liberating to own my Positivity, Woo, and Communication skills in my leadership role and to lean on others to fill the gaps. Ultimately, this meant that I formed authentic relationships that continue to have enduring benefits to this day.

I am consistently reminded of my decision to become a teacher after I graduated from college. I figured because I had been a good student and had fairly strong oral communication skills, I would be effective in the high school classroom.

While these skills gave me comfort in the environment, I did not know how to actually TEACH the students. They may have been entertained by my personality, but I am quite confident they didn't learn much from me. Perhaps if I had stayed around long enough and practiced the trade, I may have become a good teacher. Like networking, teaching isn't something you just do and are naturally good at. You must learn, practice, fail, practice again, and continually hone the craft to be effective.

JoDee's strengths as defined by Gallup[7]:

1. **Maximizer:** People who are especially talented in the Maximizer theme stimulate personal and group excellence; they seek to transform something strong into something superb.

2. **Arranger:** People who are especially talented in the Arranger theme organize with a flexibility that complements this ability. They like to figure out how all of the pieces and resources can be arranged for maximum productivity.

3. **Positivity:** People who are especially talented in the Positivity theme have an enthusiasm that is contagious. They are upbeat and can get others excited about what they are going to do.

4. **Strategic:** People who are especially talented in the Strategic theme create alternative ways to proceed. Faced with any given scenario, they can quickly spot the relevant patterns and issues.

5. **Futuristic:** People who are especially talented in the Futuristic theme are inspired by the future and what could be. They inspire others with their visions of the future.

I can think of many situations in the past where I:

- used my strengths to help me be successful
- excelled on a project by using at least one of my strengths
- had my best day because I was in my strengths zone

As an example, I was a committee member and the chair of the HR Indiana SHRM Conference for many years. As the chair of the conference, I also served on the HR Indiana SHRM state council. It was strategic for me to volunteer and a significant networking opportunity for me and my business. The state council included 40 people from all over the state of Indiana. I also networked with multiple vendors, sponsors, exhibitors, committee members, and attendees, greatly expanding my network.

Each year, I sought out ways to make the conference bigger and better by using my strengths. Here are a few examples:

- **Arranger:** I took great pride in choosing our core committee chairs. During my first year, I made numerous changes to the committee. There were people who were no longer the right person for their role due to personal or work reasons. I created stronger subcommittees. I rearranged people and roles to achieve maximum productivity for the committee.

- **Positivity:** I unquestionably led with positivity. Year after year I set goals for more attendees, more bookstore sales, and higher profits. It was not pie in the sky or wishful thinking. We set goals, made plans, and achieved the goals!
- **Strategic:** I continually strategized for myself and the committee. We never settled for repeating exactly what we had done before, even though the conference had been highly successful for 27 years. Rather, we looked for ways to earn more money, spend more efficiently, offer more learning opportunities, inspire participants with outstanding speakers, increase networking opportunities, minimize the distance to walk between sessions, and more!

Knowing our strengths helps us authentically form relationships. Using CliftonStrengths® also opens up an entire framework for knowing and appreciating the strengths of others. Instead of seeing other people as different in a negative sense, we see them as unique and strong in their own ways. This approach to knowing and valuing ourselves and others has been life changing. It is foundational to JoyPowered® networking. While we may bring our strengths forward, we also seek to listen and learn about the strengths of others.

It's always fun when we meet someone who "speaks CliftonStrengths®." They understand our language and we know immediately what unique gifts they bring to the relationship.

Great Networkers Aren't Born That Way, They Grow into It

Networking skills can be taught, and having a natural disposition to networking doesn't necessarily make you good at it. Networking comes fairly easily to me, but I am better at it in some situations than others.

When I attend a conference, I like to have a specific purpose or a combination of a few purposes. If I'm speaking at the conference, for example, my goal is usually to find additional opportunities to speak. I strive to be professional, engaging, and interesting in my presentation so that any event planners in the audience will remember me. I look for opportunities to network with the leaders of the conference and other speakers. When I network with other speakers, I try to learn from their speaking style and find out where else they have spoken before or plan to speak in the future.

Networking skills can be taught, and having a natural disposition to networking doesn't necessarily make you good at it.

At many of my speaking engagements, I know very few people in the audience, and I might only be there for my session, so trying to network with the larger group can be difficult. I love to hear the keynotes and earn continuing education credits, but these are not my priorities when I'm speaking.

As another example, I attend an annual credit union conference. My priority for this event is to learn more about credit unions and any new laws or policies and procedures impacting them. This helps me serve as a better board member for my local credit union. I love learning at this event, yet I don't feel a strong desire to network with the group. The majority of the other attendees serve on credit union boards that are significantly smaller than the one I serve on and they are likely not potential clients for my own business. I enjoy both of these types of conferences, but for very different reasons.

If you recognize the value of networking and want to learn, you can absolutely become a JoyPowered® networker.

If you recognize the value of networking and want to learn, you can absolutely become a JoyPowered® networker. It starts with knowing yourself, adopting a mindset that reflects the importance of networking, and abiding by your networking needs and identity. Whether you are an introvert or extrovert, an executive or a job seeker, a business developer or an HR manager, you can be a JoyPowered® networker. Capitalize on your natural talents, develop a strategy, practice, fail, and keep on honing it.

Key Takeaways

- **Confident networkers know themselves, and they don't try to be someone they aren't.** This doesn't mean they are done learning and evolving – just that they aren't trying to take on a persona that isn't theirs.
- **The desire to learn is key to being a JoyPowered® networker.** If you want to be a good networker, you will be.
- **Identifying the strengths of others is a great foundation for connection.** Everyone wants to be known for who they really are. Seeking to understand others' strengths and talents is a key to true connection.

2

BE STRATEGIC

There is no perfect network. Just as we need friendship, family, and professional circles, we need various communities, relationships, and networks to thrive. Some of those will be more fruitful for us, and some will be more fruitful for others.

The first thing to define for yourself is your goal in meeting a person or joining a community.

Are you looking for:

- A new career?
- Business or sales opportunities?
- Training or mentoring connections?
- Referrals?
- New friendships or relationships?

By defining what you want from the connection, you can more easily make decisions about who to connect with and how.

The Rule of Five

I once heard someone say we are the average of the five people we spend the most time with. While "average" can apply to many things – skill levels, career status, or overall likability, to name a few – it's also a fair way to think about the many ways you can connect and join with others.

For instance, in pickleball, I love to play with people who are better than me to improve my skills, with people who are about the same level as me for great competition, and with people who aren't as good as me so that I can evangelize the sport and help them improve.

In JoyPowered® networking, it's the same way. Groups serve different purposes at different times and spaces in our lives. While you may once have been part of a networking group for young professionals, you may now find yourself ready to belong to a group of emerging managers. When I first entered the workforce as a new high school teacher, I needed a mentor who could show me the ropes and help me navigate the new profession and school climate. I also needed to be around other first-year teachers who could empathize with my challenges.

Network Without Assumptions

After I left teaching, I spent several years in the Edutainment industry. I worked at a video and web production firm that developed content for teachers to use in the classroom. Our clients were The Discovery Channel, National Geographic, US News and World Report, and other very interesting content resources. I love telling the story of how I got this position.

I was watching the local news one night and there was a report that The Discovery Channel was moving their headquarters to Silver Spring, Maryland. I had the big idea that I wanted to go work for them developing teacher materials. I got the name of the CEO from my mother, who was serving on the Maryland State Board of Education, and the next day, I sent a letter to her. She never replied.

The next week, I was talking to a friend on the phone and told her about my goal. She said, "Hold on. I'm having takeout with a friend who works at TDC and she can tell you who to contact." That friend got on the phone, gave me the name and number of the production company that TDC outsourced their Cable in the Classroom development to, and told me to call the next day once she had a chance to tell them about me. A few weeks later, I was invited to be in some focus groups. A year later, I was hired. This ended up being a 10-year relationship.

I tell this story because it is a great example of networking without assumptions. I had no way of knowing that my friend had a connection at The Discovery Channel, but she was within the circle of moms and educators that I trusted. I also didn't tell her about my goal with the intention that she would connect me or find me a job. I was just sharing a dream.

> You never know where a resource or connection may come from.

You never know where a resource or connection may come from. It never entered my mind that a fellow mom who was doing some home tutoring may have a connection of value. I've embraced this mindset ever since. I listen openly and share openly. I also try not to prejudge a situation or a person. This isn't easy. My own life has led me to biases and assumptions that I instinctively make, but I try to set them aside when I'm given the privilege of another person sharing openly and listening to me.

Don't Dismiss Anyone

Later in my career, I ended up tapping into my writing talents to become a content marketer and strategist. Essentially, I learned how to write for an audience. Whether my client was a data consultant or a software as a service (SaaS) vendor, I would seek to understand the problems they solved and for whom they solved them. Then, I would interpret those problems and solutions in more approachable language.

This opportunity led me to move completely out of the education space and into corporate. It happened in part because of the confidence I gained in my own writing skills over the years, but also because of the people I met along the way. I met many of these people through my kids' schools, sports, my church, and my neighborhood. While we rarely talked about my profession, I was able to develop mutual relationships of trust that resulted in connections and ultimately job opportunities.

My point is don't dismiss anyone, but don't be too focused on what you can get from the relationship either. If you're always open to knowing more about someone and sharing more about yourself, you will have choices you can make along the way, and those choices will feed you personally, professionally, socially, and perhaps spiritually.

Pay It Forward

> When you consider finding the right networks, relationships, and communities, remember that it may not only be about you.

I recognize that I have been very lucky in my career path and I try to pay that good fortune forward. A single conversation with a fellow mom landed me a job with a production company and changed the entire trajectory of my life. I want to be able to do this for others. I make a commitment to myself and to anyone I engage with to listen and to not forget what they say and what wants or needs I might be able to help them with. Oftentimes that may be a simple introduction or an idea that leads to another idea.

When you consider finding the right networks, relationships, and communities, remember that it may not only be about you. Sometimes you are the giver, not the receiver, of the benefits of the relationship. Think of the age-old adage that what goes around comes around, or even the pay-it-forward mindset. In either case, it's just part of healthy relationship building to include relationships that may not be equal. You'd be surprised what you can learn from someone who may not be as _____ as you are. (fill in that blank with anything: "good a pickleball player," "successful," "intelligent," "socially adept," etc.) Not only do you reap the benefit of feeling good about helping someone along, but you may also find that you reap other benefits outside the expected parameters of the relationship.

My story here, like many others I share, comes from the pickleball court. I slowly forged a friendship with a guy on the court, not knowing anything about his line of work. Eventually, my husband and I became friends with him and his wife, and one day he asked if I could help him craft a bio for his new real estate business. This small request (reciprocated with a bottle of wine) resulted in an enduring friendship and professional relationship. He's been our realtor and he's hired me and my daughters for some marketing work. You just never know who will need you and how. Keep an open mind.

Sometimes You Have to Be Selective

Now that I've suggested being totally open to all kinds of relationships and networks, I also want to say that it's not only okay, but important to be selective. You will burn yourself out if you try to commit to too many people or communities. You won't be any good to them, and they won't be any good to you. I am no longer affiliated with any education communities, because I don't bring any value to them or receive any value from them anymore. I also have to say no to individuals sometimes because I don't have capacity. I try to make sure that's done with love, knowing that I will assuredly come up short in meeting any expectations for mutual benefits.

> You will burn yourself out if you try to commit to too many people or communities.

Earlier I mentioned my role leading the conference committee on the HR Indiana SHRM State Council. This role led me to long-term friendships, business opportunities for Purple Ink, and top talent who joined our team or our clients' teams. I spent a significant amount of time serving in this capacity, but in 2023, it was time to step back. I wanted others to have the opportunity to lead and grow like I did and to offer some new thoughts and ideas to improve the conference.

So, how do you assess the value of a business relationship, network, or community? Here are some guiding principles about being strategic and JoyPowered® in your networking relationships.

1. Meaning, value, and JoyPower come from receiving and giving. As you assess the strategic value of any relationship or community, try to look at it from all angles. Are you learning? Are you teaching? Are you giving (referrals, jobs, knowledge, mentoring)? Are you receiving (connections, opportunities)?

2. No single person or group will meet all your needs. Just as you turn to different friends for different needs, you should not put all your networking eggs in one basket. Perhaps you affiliate with one group to stay current on industry trends, another to learn strategies for growing your business, and yet another to diversify your geographic reach.

3. Don't spread yourself too thin. The worst thing you can do in joining groups is to commit (and sometimes pay) to be part of the group and then not put in the work it takes to reap value. I say this to folks who look to join Powered by Purple Ink. It is not for the solopreneur who is too busy to invest in others. It takes a commitment of time and energy to get to know the others within the community so that they will also seek to know you. If you do not have the bandwidth for it, it is time to sever ties.

A Note About Acquaintances, Friends, and Business Relationships

Just as we make deliberate and strategic choices about which groups to participate in, we also make choices about whom to spend time with. While some of our time is dedicated to specific projects and people, we have choices about which people to be around and how and when to be with others. This is as important, if not more so, than the groups we choose to join. I will not tell you who to be friends with, but I have some strong feelings about the criteria I use for investing in relationships.

Here are a few questions I ask myself to gauge the level of commitment I can and should be making in a relationship.

1. Am I curious about this person? If so, I will absolutely meet them, but that may be the end of the relationship. I still commit to remembering them, as they gave their time and told me their story.

2. Is this person curious about me? If so, I will share authentically and concisely in the context of our new relationship. I will also try to assess the mutual benefits of knowing one another.

3. Do I have something of value I can give this person? Even if I simply have a resource or a connection I can share, I still try to be discerning about whether it's worth it. I know this sounds harsh, but if the relationship isn't moving forward, then maybe we should just share gratitude for the time and move on. But if I have something that I think could be of value to the person AND I think we have more than a single meeting in us, I give generously.

4. Does knowing this person improve my life? This is a big question. As a curious extrovert, I often find people very interesting, but interesting and edifying are two different things. To interest me just takes a single exchange. To edify requires a sustained relationship. This is a bit of a tipping point for me. I try to assess whether my life will be better off by continuing to know this person. It may be that I care about their trajectory and my life is improved by continuing to give to them. I think about a few relationships I have that may look one-sided from the outside, but I derive so much joy from being present for and with these people that I am truly uplifted. And, of course,

there is great edification when I can learn from or grow with another person.

5. Is this one of those magical connections? Some people are worth everything you've got to stay connected. Sometimes you can see this right away, and other times it takes a little while, but when you find those gems, you know you've got to make the time, invest the energy, and show up. JoDee is one of those gems for me! I knew it early on and have reaffirmed this many times over.

Key Takeaways

- **Many factors (geography, age, career path, etc.) influence our decisions about which communities we participate in and when.** Take inventory regularly and only participate in groups that are relevant and add value to your life.

- **While it is great to be curious and interested in others, you do not have time or capacity to invest in everyone you meet.** Be discerning and devote your energies according to standards you have chosen about value and meaning.

- **JoyPowered® networking is strategic.** It is not a broad, sweeping, meet-everyone approach to networking. It is discerning and mutual.

3

STOP WAITING FOR JOYPOWERED® NETWORKING TO HAPPEN

Many times, we are waiting for someone else to make the first move, whether that move is inviting us to lunch or to join a conversation. People wait for their boss, their peers, or leadership to change their situation for them. If you want to be a JoyPowered® networker, you have to be intentional in making it happen for yourself.

> If you want to be a JoyPowered® networker, you have to be intentional in making it happen for yourself.

Joy is a choice in the moment. There will always be something that we are excitedly or reluctantly waiting for, but let's focus on choosing joy today.

One of my favorites, Dr. Seuss, concurs:

"The Waiting Place...for people just waiting. Waiting for a train to go or a bus to come, or a plane to go or the mail to come, or the rain to go or the phone to ring, or the snow to snow or waiting around for a Yes or No or waiting for their hair to grow. Everyone is just waiting. Waiting for the fish to bite or waiting for the wind to fly

a kite or waiting around for Friday night or waiting, perhaps, for their Uncle Jake, or a pot to boil, or a Better Break, or a string of pearls, or a pair of pants, or a wig with curls, or Another Chance. Everyone is just waiting."

—*Oh, the Places You'll Go!*

Stop waiting and start networking. Only then can you discover what works best for you so that you attain your goal AND discover joy in doing so.

This will look different for everyone who reads this book. Maybe the last time you tried to network it didn't go so well because you had the wrong intention or purpose. This time, with a different intention or purpose, you may find different results. If our stories can inspire you to stop waiting and start finding joy, we have done our job.

My Networking Journey: Show Up, Have Fun, and Make Time for It!

My mom told me many times how afraid she was when I went to kindergarten. She said my siblings were ready academically and socially, but that I held onto her knee and hid behind her for the first five years of my life. Despite her initial fears, she laughed when she shared that when she dropped me off that first day, she never saw me again.

I am not sure what happened that day, what engaged me. I do not remember a time when I hid behind anyone. My memory says I have always been gregarious. Of course, I had the typical junior high awkwardness, but I always had lots of friends, family, cousins, and neighbors around. I felt completely comfortable going to a college where I only knew a handful of people. I was ready to explore, to meet new people, and to network!

Was I strategic in meeting people in college? I am not sure. I knew I wanted to meet people, so I joined the accounting club, the dance team, and a sorority. I was covering my profession, my fun activity, and my social goals. Today, I continue to use this pattern of participating in groups that involve my profession, fun activities, and social goals.

My first job was in a public accounting firm of 1,000 people, but our office only included about 100 people. I was surrounded by people, many of whom are still my friends now. It was natural. It was easy. We went to lunch, to corporate training sessions, and to social events on the weekends together. We respected each other, and we were driven by the same goal: becoming partners in this firm. Almost everyone I worked with at that time was under 30, and we did networking at its finest. These people later became clients, mentors, advisors, recruits, and referral sources.

I was just having fun. I was not being strategic – or was I?

Make Time for Networking

In the first few years of my professional career, I was active in the Indiana CPA Society because one of the partners asked me to take a role on her committee. I joined the Junior League because another friend said it was fun and a great way to meet people. I took on community leadership roles and I joined the board of our local Big Brothers Big Sisters.

My managers and directors were very supportive of my activities. They paid the membership dues, and it became a part of my "timed work activities." It was encouraged and supported. I was evaluated on my involvement in the community, praised for it, and encouraged to do it.

My involvement in community activities continued over the years. I made time to serve in volunteer roles. My coworkers and the board members of organizations I served became social friends as well. I got involved in my church, where I attended random dinner nights with parishioners I didn't know and met more new people. Over the years, many people have asked me, "How do you have the time to volunteer so much?" My answer is always, "How do you not make the time? There are so many opportunities."

In 2000, I transferred to Indianapolis, four times the size of Evansville, the city I'd been living in. I knew many of the folks in the Indianapolis office and my sister and her family lived there, so I knew I had a base to grow from.

By this point in my career, my daughter was entering first grade. Who knew that a significant part of my new Indy-area network would be the parents at her elementary school? When my four-year-old son started playing soccer, bam! A whole new world of connections developed in kids' sports.

Our idea of what networking is or could be usually does not start with four- and six-year-olds, but it jump-started my network in a way I would never have dreamed. We do not have to be the president of a professional association to explore new connections (although it's a good option!). We can be moms, dads, sisters, brothers, and neighbors. We can build our networks in a way that fits into our lives naturally. I had the blessing of having a lot of flexibility, so I seized multiple opportunities to volunteer in my kids' activities as a room parent, PTO board member, soccer mom, Brownie troop volunteer, etc.

So many people I talk to say they do not have time to volunteer or to do things outside of work, much less network. If we see it as a step outside of our normal flow of work, pets, children, and more, it becomes just one more thing we have to do. If we see it as more fully living in the flow of work, then it is an expansion, an opportunity we can incorporate seamlessly.

> We can build our networks in a way that fits into our lives naturally.

Networking as a Business Owner

The big life-changing moment in my networking journey was on June 3, 2010, the day of incorporation of my HR consulting business,

Purple Ink. This was the day that the rubber met the road for my network. I needed to turn to the network I had built to find people who could help me – hire me, refer me, support me. Who in my network could I refer or go to for advice? Would they refer me to their friends and networks? This is the day that networking went from fun to a necessity for the success of my business.

I remained committed to activities I enjoyed that could be good networking outlets: boards, parent groups, church, etc. To be clear, I did not get involved in church activities because I thought I would find clients. I got involved because I knew I would meet new people, build relationships, and discover friends. My passion for volunteering and networking eventually led to client referrals, new clients, candidates for jobs with our recruiting clients, and so much more.

I built my business, and they hired me, referred me, supported me – and more! Years later, I still get phone calls and emails from people who say, "You might not remember me, but I was in your class at University of Evansville, I served on a board with you, our kids played soccer (or cross country or rugby or track or swimming or lacrosse) together, and I have been following you on Facebook, LinkedIn, or someone just told me that…"

My greatest fear in starting my own business was not about finances or getting new clients. It was about working from home alone. I was terrified thinking that my husband and kids would leave for work and school and that I would be left alone, possibly without anything to do. This really forced me to reach out to my network and make some phone calls. I started with, "Hey, I started my own consulting company, Purple Ink, and I would love to take some time to learn about what you are doing and share what I am building."

Purple Ink is now a thriving business, and I continue to network in a similar fashion, by volunteering in my church, in my profession, and in personal passions. I am involved in the National Association of Women Business Owners, Executive Women in Finance, a local credit union board, and the National Speakers Association and served many years as a leader in our local SHRM chapter and State Council. They are very different groups from those I was involved in 10 to15 years ago and from those I was involved in 25 to 30 years ago. I serve on different committees or leadership roles at church. It's not soccer moms and school volunteering anymore, and it is definitely not playing kickball.

Key Takeaways

- **A great network requires that you take the first steps.** People will not just come to you because you are awesome. You need to be proactive to build a great network.
- **JoyPowered® networking is a process that evolves over time and with experience.** Your approach and your network of people will change over time. Embrace those changes.
- **Different networks serve different purposes.** You may have multiple networks for different roles you fill. They may or may not overlap. Be adaptable and make time for all of them.

4

KNOW WHEN TO HOLD AND WHEN TO FOLD

I had a friend in college ask me if we were "divorcing" when our friend- ship seemed to be slipping away. I was taken aback by her question (and still think it may have been a little overdramatic), but I understood that she wanted closure. I think the same needs apply to our business relationships and the communities we choose to align ourselves with.

As I mentioned, I started my professional life as a high school teacher. I chose the field because I had been a good student, thought of myself as an engaging communicator, and liked the idea of having summers off. I did not last long in this job as I quickly realized that being an effective teacher is far different from being an entertaining communicator in front of a captive audience. High schoolers aren't especially captive (at least not voluntarily), and a classroom usually consists of a wide range of learning abilities. My engaging personality only went so far, and after two years in the classroom, I accepted defeat and moved on.

I needed a community of educators to support me during those years, and I no longer needed that community when I chose a different path. I still value the wisdom and relationships that came from that time, though. I learned about the various "stakeholders" in the field of education (teachers, students, families, administration, community, etc.), the variety of effective strategies for teaching, and the relationship between schools, politics, community, economics, and more. This knowledge has continued to serve me as I became a parent, changed jobs, and then served as a school governing board chair.

My point?

Don't ever forget what you've learned and who taught you.

While your perspective may change, you still have a great foundation to build on. I no longer need to be part of a community of educators or young moms, even though some very strong friendships and learning arose from those affiliations. So, even if I have decided to "divorce" a person or a group, I can and should still take what I learned from them as I move on.

> Don't ever forget what you've learned and who taught you.

Think about the many groups you have been a part of in your personal life and career. Perhaps you have been part of groups in industry, local networking, education, church, school, parenting, hobby, sports, etc. These groups shift over time based upon your age, lifestyle, geography, career path, and interests.

For illustration purposes, let me share some of the groups I was in when I was 35, 48, and now at 57:

AGE 35	AGE 48	AGE 57
Lived in Maryland and worked as a content developer for an educational video/web production company	*Lived in Indiana and worked as a freelance content marketer*	*Live in North Carolina and provide marketing/sales/strategic leadership for a national network*

Church moms group	School governing board and sports team parents	Powered by Purple Ink (national network of workforce consultants)
United States Tennis Association (Maryland teams)	United States Tennis Association (Indiana teams)	Cape Fear Pickleball Club
Educational Writer's Association	Marketing meetups	Society for Human Resource Management
Neighborhood	Multiple industry business communities (SaaS and marketing primarily)	Business book writing community
Maryland book club	Indiana book club	North Carolina book club

Not only did my children and I age, but I moved states, changed jobs (and my preferred racquet sport), and expanded my professional network. I'm sure you can see the evolution of your own interests and career paths over the years, as well. Whether you've aged out of a group, moved locations, or changed industries or roles, you are not the same person with the same needs as you were five or ten years ago.

It is a great idea to take inventory of your affiliations (and relationships) periodically to assess the mutual value of each. I could do a similar exercise and track my closest friends or business relationships at each stage of my life, and there would be some crossover, but there would also be lots of turnover. It's natural and vital to our growth and ability to be relevant in our networking efforts.

Key Takeaways

- **You control your choices.** While it did not feel good to have my college buddy ask me if we were 'divorcing," I realized that I had some control and responsibility to determine if I was in or out. I owed it to myself and to her to decide whether I was willing to remain committed to the friendship. If you deem a relationship or a community no longer valuable, then move on, and do so deliberately and with love.

- **Choose JoyPowered® relationships and communities that feed you and that you feed** (remember the rule of five). Always seek to give and receive from a network.

- **Don't be too quick to judge how valuable a new connection will be.** Keep an open mind, listen well, and share honestly. You never know where an opportunity will come from – either to give or receive a benefit.

- **Allow for some flexibility in your relationships.** What you thought you might get from a relationship or experience may evolve into something very different if you are flexible.

- **Do not overextend yourself with too many people, communities, and networks.** Know your capacity and serve well those with whom you have chosen to affiliate. Meet your own expectations and theirs.

- **Be proactive in your decisions about affiliations.** Do not wait for people to reach out to include you. Do your homework about groups that will meet your current criteria for networking and get involved.

5

TIMING AND TRUST

Networking is NOT a single, coincidental meeting, although it CAN start that way.

Timing

In 13 years of business, I have never made a cold sales call, and have only made one warm one. Before I quit my full-time role to start my business, I made a phone call to a CEO who was a client of both of the CPA firms I had worked with. I asked for his opinion, not for work. "If I was to start an HR consulting business, what types of services might you be interested in?" I was trying to decide which services and how many I wanted to offer and truly wanted his input. Of course, it was also a way to let him know that I was starting my own firm. His response was, "Our Executive HR Director just resigned. When can you start?" I quit my job the next day, and Purple Ink began.

Sometimes, we just hit pay dirt. We meet someone who needs what we can offer or someone we already know is looking for something we can provide. That does not mean we can just sit back and wait for those moments to happen. We have to be intentional in making good decisions and putting ourselves in positions that favor good outcomes. We keep networking with intention and strategy to create those opportunities.

There are many different ways to make those opportunities happen.

Networking can be a physical meeting, or it might be a LinkedIn post, a newsletter, or a phone or video call. It might be scheduled or random. For example, I was on a webinar and noticed a client was in attendance as well. I reached out to them via a direct message to say hello and to set up a follow-up meeting.

Connections May Come In and Out of Your Life and Career

In 1988, I joined a committee in the Indiana CPA Society. I was just three years out of college and drove two and a half hours to the big city to attend my first meeting. When I arrived for the meeting, I realized I was at least 10 years younger than anyone else on the committee. My thoughts and experiences were very helpful to the committee, though, because we were focused on attracting students to get their CPA licenses.

The chair of the committee, Mark, was very impressive. He worked for a big global accounting firm, had loads of experience in recruiting at college campuses, and seemed to know everyone! I served on this committee with him for only a year, and we only met live two times. In 2000, I moved to Indianapolis, and our paths crossed again in 2006. He lived and worked in Indianapolis, and he was the benefits broker for my new firm. He didn't remember me, but I remembered him and sought out opportunities to work with and learn from him.

As I write this in 2023, Mark is back in the accounting profession and serves as my tax advisor. He is also a long-time mentor and friend of mine. The more I got to know him, the more I knew he was a person I wanted to have in my professional network. When I met him in 1988, I did not realize how much of an interest he would have in my perspective and work. As it turns out, he has been a client, a source of advice, an idea generator, a tax advisor, a collaborator, and a good friend for many years.

First-Day Impressions Matter

On my first day of work after college, February 25, 1985, I met a senior accountant, Joe, whose cubicle was next to mine. February 25th is NOT a good day to begin your career in public accounting. Everyone else was deep into "busy season" and they did not have time to train a newbie. They forgot I was starting that day, so I did not have a clean desk. My desk drawers were locked and no one could find the key, no one greeted me, and no one took me to lunch.

At 5 p.m., no one moved. At 6 p.m., no one moved. At 6:30 p.m., my "cubicle neighbor," Joe, stood on his chair and peeked over the cubicle and said, "You can go home whenever you want." I grabbed my purse and coat and ran to my car crying. That's a story for a different book, but I knew right then that I had someone who was watching out for me. Joe is still a mentor for me today. He has been a referral source, an idea generator, a podcast guest, an accountability partner, a business advisor, and a friend.

Even Good-Natured Teasing Can Turn into an Enduring Friendship

Within the first 15 months of my career, I attended training at our corporate office in Indianapolis. Tom, our firm's HR Director, welcomed each of us to the training. As we went around the room to introduce ourselves, Tom very loudly exclaimed, "Jo Dee? Is that like Jim Bob?" Some might have been taken aback, but I just laughed. It felt like when I went to college and immediately was called "JoDee from Loogootee" (for those of you who are unfamiliar with Southern Indiana, "JoDee" and "Loogootee" rhyme)! It was a call out to me. It became a connection point. It became something that others remembered about me. No one forgot me that week.

That made it easier to stay connected with the group on a long-term basis. Tom certainly never forgot my name and we developed a friendship. I felt comfortable reaching out to him. He looked for me when he traveled to our office. I found more passion by volunteering for HR assignments like recruiting and training, allowing me to ultimately gravitate to a full-time role in HR instead of accounting. Tom was the first person who nudged me into consulting. He has been a friend, leader, mentor, and advisor to me ever since.

What was it that stood out to me about these three mentors throughout my career? I am not sure I could have described this back then, but looking back, I realize how very different their styles were. My goal was to learn the best – or my favorite – styles, techniques, and words from each of them and mold them into my own unique style. I knew that each of them advocated for me. They listened to me. Rarely did they tell me exactly what to do, but they gave me different ideas and different perspectives on issues.

I had no idea back then that they would be important for me after 40 years. I met all of them between 1985 and 1988, and each of them later became a crucial advisor to me through changing employers, starting my business, hiring new people, succession planning, and much more. Their thoughts and opinions are important to me, even though I did not always follow their advice! Over the course of 39 years, these three keep popping in and out of my career, and I am hoping they will continue to do so.

> In JoyPowered® networking your circle grows.

Trust

In JoyPowered® networking your circle grows. You'll meet all kinds of people to know, develop relationships with, expand business with, learn from, and more. It is wonderful to have an extensive circle of people that you can turn to for a variety of needs. However, even though you will inevitably grow the size of your personal network, you do NOT want to sacrifice quality for quantity, and you always want to seek to develop trusting relationships with key individuals.

So, how do you identify who you should trust and who you should want to trust you?

Once Burned, Always Shy

Have you ever had your trust broken? Put yourself out there and been disappointed by someone? I have. And it does not feel so good.

One example I can think of was when I was given an opportunity to interview for a great job at the Smithsonian Institute. The woman who interviewed me told me how much she liked me and my resume and pretty much promised me the job. I never heard from her again. As it turns out, she left the department shortly after the interview and never told me. When I finally reached another person in the department, she told me the position had been filled. I was devastated. I wanted that job badly and trusted that the woman I met with would hire me. I had been introduced to her by a family member, so I figured she was trustworthy.

As I look back on that experience, I wonder why I trusted her so quickly. It was probably two reasons: she had been connected to me through someone I trusted, and I wanted to trust her because I wanted the job very badly. As disappointed as I was, the experience did alter my willingness to trust my gut on these types of experiences. From that point on, I have told myself that it is not a sure thing until I get my first paycheck.

We use our own life experiences to gauge the character of new people we meet. If we've been burned in the past, we may assume that will happen again. If we meet someone with a familiar style or attitude, we will likely trust or distrust them based upon our previous relationships with others.

> Circles of trust can be formed over time and with a variety of roots.

I think it's reasonable to learn from past experiences and to trust our gut, but that's not enough when it comes to meeting and networking with new people. Circles of trust can be formed over time and with a variety of roots.

When I think about my trust circle, a few people come to mind.

Observing Integrity and Wisdom

I met Steve when he was brought in to run operations for a startup I was consulting with. His reputation as a successful business owner and a man of deep integrity preceded him. Within the first few days of his arrival, I watched him listen intently to everyone within the company. As I grew to know him as a leader, I found him to be discerning, honest, sensitive, and willing to lead in difficult times. I felt fortunate to work with him and knew I wanted him in my permanent inner circle, so when the business was sold and we were no longer working with one another, I made a point to stay connected. I'd regularly reach out to him to have coffee or meet up with him and his wife to keep the relationship alive. While we no longer work together or really see one another, I know without a doubt that I could call Steve at any time to ask for a professional favor, and he would help me if he could.

Connecting with Connectors

Mike is one of those guys who knows everyone. We first met when he took his daughters on the same Haiti mission trip that I took my daughter on. It was a bonding experience, for sure. Shared experiences like these can be very powerful in building trust and enduring friendships. While our paths crossed here and there, it wasn't until we served on the same school governing board that I decided Mike would be part of my inner circle. The irony here is that we had some pretty tough disagreements about subjects we felt very strongly about. Over the years, I had to earn Mike's trust so that ultimately, we would both be willing to help one another out, make referrals and introductions, and support one another. The reason Mike is part of my inner circle of trust is because he's honest and passionate and would do anything for someone he cares about.

Trust Goes Both Ways

Tierra was a young mom living in a residential home for unwed moms when I became her mentor. We spent two years in this relationship. During that time, we grew very close, sharing many experiences: celebrations, trainings, navigating jobs and childcare, and more. When Tierra moved out of the house, it became much more difficult for us to have a steady and trusting relationship. Not only did we not see one another as regularly, but Tierra also had a lot more to deal with and couldn't always be honest with me about things going on in her life. While we ultimately discontinued our mentor/mentee relationship because of a variety of factors, including a loss of trust, I would say that Tierra remains an influencer and connector in my life. Because of our relationship, I am more aware of the plight of women in poverty and the challenges they face. While Tierra is not a close friend of mine, I consider her part of my network because she has impacted my thinking and I remain a resource for her.

Key Takeaways

As you meet people, you may need a set of criteria by which to measure that person's trustworthiness and value in your network. Here are some thoughts to ponder:

- Have you witnessed them in action and observed qualities you admire?
- Do their stories align with what you've researched or learned about them?
- Do they communicate values that align with yours?
- Are they honest with you?
- Do they follow through on their commitments to you?
- Has the relationship stood the test of time? Even if it has morphed, is it significant?
- Is this relationship mutual? If not, is there value that you should be providing as part of your goal to be giving and receiving in all valuable relationships?

6

JOYPOWERED® NETWORKING REQUIRES PRACTICE

We are not all at ease with all the skills involved in effective networking and relationship building. Some of you may be downright afraid of networking. Some of you may think you've got it down. Some of you may know it's a necessary evil and are open to some coaching. Let me just say that whether you are a *natural* or not, we all have to practice the craft.

> Let me just say that whether you are a *natural* or not, we all have to practice the craft.

Let me give you a pickleball model:

I've played tennis since I was six years old. I know how to make contact between a ball and a racquet, and I know how to cover a court. Some might think I would be a natural at pickleball. However, when I first grabbed a paddle, I swung and missed. After I had played for a while, I would regularly make unforced errors and didn't have the greatest strategic approach to the game. While some might say I was a good player, I knew I was lacking the consistency and finesse needed to be really good. I know what is needed now. I just need to practice those skills so I stop making the unforced errors and master the strategic shots – like the third shot drop and forcing open spaces.

If you have the fundamental belief that networking is something you want or need to be good at professionally, then you'll accept that you need practice to become good at it, even if you think you have the natural talents to do it well.

Tapping Your Strengths to Network

Let's consider how understanding what you do best can help you understand your own natural networking capabilities and possible areas for improvement.

I'll give you some examples of how I use my strengths in networking situations:

WOO: people with the gift of "winning others over" are generally comfortable in a large group of people even if they don't know anyone. I frequently attend networking events, conferences, and meetings where I don't know anyone. I assume that most of the other people also don't know a lot of people, and it is easy for me to start up a conversation that makes both of us feel more comfortable.

Strategic: Whether I am attending a large event or meeting with someone one-on-one, I like to prepare a plan first. It's typically in my head and not actually written, but writing could work as well. I think about:

1. Who do I want to meet?
2. What are some great starter questions?
3. What might I request of them? (even if the ask might be down the road and not in this initial conversation)
4. Whom would I like them to introduce me to?
5. Whom might I introduce them to?
6. What do I want them to know about me or my business?

Futuristic: this strength helps me to think ahead. Here's how it typically shows up:

1. I connect on LinkedIn with people I know will be in the meeting or at the event.
2. I take the lead in following up with the people I am most interested in or with those to whom I made a commitment.

Communication and Connectedness are in my top five CliftonStrengths®.

According to Gallup:

"People exceptionally talented in the Communication theme generally find it easy to put their thoughts into words. They are good conversationalists and presenters."

"People exceptionally talented in the Connectedness theme have faith in the links among all things. They believe there are few coincidences and that almost every event has meaning."[7]

These two strengths fuel my networking practice. Because I am comfortable expressing myself and believe there are no coincidences, I see every person I meet and connect with as an opportunity to *find* meaning – and hopefully, to *give* meaning.

While these strengths enable my networking, they must be honed and practiced – like my third shot drop in pickleball. If I get too caught up in the expressive part of my Communication strength, I can lose the opportunity to listen and remember others' stories. If I seek too deep a meaning in all new relationships, I may become overwhelmed with so many connections that I cannot tend to all of them well.

Every Strength Has a Shadow Side

What are your natural strengths? Have you ever noticed that those same strengths can sometimes be weaknesses? For example:

> I have Positivity and Self-Assurance in my top 10 CliftonStrengths®. Basically, I tend to expect everyone and everything to be good, and I feel confident in that. Therefore, I naturally assume that most people will want to network with me, will enjoy talking to me, and will want to learn more about me and my business. Sound like a big assumption? Of course, this could be good or bad. It does give me the confidence to network, but I might go a little overboard.
>
> I also have the Input strength in my top 10. Per Gallup, "people who are especially talented in this theme have a craving to know more. Often they like to collect and archive all kinds of information."[7] This strength drives me to read, to travel, and to ask lots of questions. This, of course, can also lead me to ask too many questions. The person I am talking to may not be interested in sharing more or in answering a lot of questions at one time. I have to be particularly self-aware to know when to stop.

Perhaps you are an analytical person who thinks critically about ideas when someone is talking. You may even have some great ideas you would like to share with a person when you meet for the first time. But what if those ideas are seen as skepticism or a lack of support? Perhaps you will want to consider saving some of those ideas for a future encounter after the relationship has grown in maturity and can handle your analysis. Maybe you need to pause to discern whether the timing is right or the person is ready to receive your analysis.

Maybe you are someone who has Command in their top five strengths. Those with Command generally have a presence and can easily take control of a situation. While this strength can be very valuable in leadership, it can be overwhelming in a one-on-one networking situation. Others may feel insignificant or threatened by your presence. You may want to work on being more approachable and listening for opportunities to lift others up. Even with Command, you can take control of a first meeting in a way that provides a framework for making the most of the meeting for both parties. It is okay to be in charge, but doing so with sensitivity is something worth practicing. It will pay dividends in the long term as you build trust with new people who may need some help navigating the meeting without feeling overwhelmed.

This self-awareness is vital to being a good networker. As we talked about in Chapter 1, knowing yourself is the first step. Now we must know both our strengths and the potential shadow sides of those strengths so that we can bring the best versions of ourselves for JoyPowered® networking.

Design Your Best Approach to Networking

Because we each have different personalities and strengths that we bring to our networking, it can be helpful to have a disciplined approach to networking. Here is mine:

1. **Seek to learn first.** While many first introductions involve some small talk, I try very hard to invite the other person to talk about themselves first. Because I believe that most people are more comfortable talking about themselves, I think allowing this to happen puts them at ease and also allows me to practice my listening.

2. **Commit to remembering people.** If I have a scheduled meeting with someone new, I tell them upfront that I make a commitment to not forget anyone. I usually do some homework ahead of time about their geography and work, and then I listen to what they wish to share. I take notes about what they say and any questions or additions I have. I think about who they

might want to meet and what content might be helpful for them. Only after they feel as though they have been heard and have shared amply do I pause and see if they invite me to share my story.

3. **Share based upon what you hear others share.** I try to be agile and concise, tailoring what I share to what they shared. If there isn't an obvious alignment between our work or backgrounds, I share a short story about what I do and why I do it. While I do want to be interesting to them, what I really want is for them to become curious and want to know even more about my work – and possible synergies. So, I try to be equally engaging and brief. This takes a lot of practice! Rambling is NOT networking, and it can be downright annoying to others. Learning how to value others' time and still be thorough in sharing the most relevant things about yourself is a critical key to JoyPowered® networking.

> Learning how to value others' time and still be thorough in sharing the most relevant things about yourself is a critical key to JoyPowered® networking.

4. **Follow up... if it is appropriate.** If this is just meant to be a one-time meetup, I accept that. However, if I sense that there is a potential future value to either of us, I try to preserve the thread and follow up with an email. Following up just to tell them that you enjoyed the connection goes a long way. Then they have your contact information for any future need.

5. **Seek to continuously learn.** There are many people out there who have studied different aspects of networking, and I want to learn from them.

Some Pros I've Learned From

While JoDee and I think we have nailed JoyPowered® networking, we both continuously learn from others about how to be more effective in creating opportunities for real connection.

Let me introduce you to some of those experts.

Vern Schellenger

I met Vern through a mutual professional acquaintance who suggested we talk. When we got on our video call, Vern was seated in his Naples home office with the plantation shutters open behind him. He was instantly congenial and warm. We had an easy and mutual first connection and realized we had a shared interest in networking. Using Vern's terminology, we both sought to learn and give. We knew there was value in staying connected, even if we didn't know exactly what that would look like. Since our first connection, I've learned a great deal from Vern about the craft of networking by taking his Networking Competency Assessment[8], reading *Strategic Connections*[9], and pondering the eight core competencies from the curriculum. In fact, JoDee and I used his curriculum as a resource for this book. Vern has helped me take what I've learned from my own experiences and turn it into practical advice for others.

Tom Kuegler and Jen Slagle

While I had a LinkedIn account two years ago, I did not use the platform much at all – much less write any posts. When we launched Powered by Purple Ink, I decided I should learn more about it as a networking tool. I spent the first few months just dabbling, adding a few connections here and there, and then I decided to dive in and learn from the pros. I participated in two of Tom Kuegler's 30-day LinkedIn Sprints where he teaches best practices for posting content and growing your network organically. Then I took a four-week course with Jen Slagle about how to refine your profile, settings, connection approach, and more. Learning from these two pros has been an excellent experience. I now post daily, have grown my network eightfold in just over a year and a half, and am connected with people who share my interest in networking and my alignment with the people profession. Tom and Jen are not the only LinkedIn gurus out there. There are many who are actively studying and testing the algorithms and offer packaged courses as well as cohorts you can join. I highly recommend finding a pro that you trust and learning directly from them.

Gavin Pringle

When it comes to the skills involved in networking, many of them are soft, such as listening, empathizing, encouraging, and expressing. These skills may come naturally to some, but they can also be learned and practiced. My friend Gavin Pringle believes in this so much that he started a company called JAKAPA. In a nutshell, JAKAPA is a training tool for soft skills.[10] I will not go into full detail on Gavin's product, but he lists a lot of soft skills that we need to be able to communicate effectively and build meaningful relationships.

Gavin's model is another way of looking at yourself and assessing the communication skills you need to be better at networking. He believes that these skills can be learned, so do not fret if they are not natural for you. There are many coaches out there (like the ones in our network, Powered by Purple Ink) who can help you develop these skills.

Key Takeaways

- **Even your strengths can be weaknesses if you do not practice using them.** Just because something is a natural talent of yours does not mean you are always using it effectively. Know your audience and setting and use the skills you need at the right time.
- **Tap the experts who know more than you do.** If you do not know how to connect, converse, add value, ask for a referral, show expertise, build a profile that attracts others, or any other networking skill, find someone who does and learn from them.

7

FOLLOW THE SPARKS

I get a lot of requests to meet with people. "Hey, JoDee, my sister is looking for a new job. Can you meet with her?" "My neighbor wants to start her own business. Can you give her some ideas?" "I'm not sure I'm in the right position to utilize my strengths. Let me buy you a cup of coffee."

I'm flattered and honored that they respect my advice, want my ideas, or want to learn from me, but if I took all these meetings, it would take at least 20 hours a week. COVID provided me the opportunity to hop on a quick phone or video call instead of driving somewhere and feeling like since I traveled there the meeting needed to last an hour. It saved me time, but I still could not say yes to everyone.

I have to make choices about whom I meet with. Sometimes I am right and sometimes I am wrong.

A few decision-tree questions I use to make these decisions:

1. Am I available? If they're only in the area for a few days or hours and I'm not available while they are here, I might offer to set up a short phone call.
2. Is this a learning opportunity for someone else on my team? If so, I connect the person with them.
3. Do I understand what this person is looking for? Can I assist them in meeting their purpose?

4. Is this a favor for someone who is or might be a strong connection for future referrals or work?

How to Request a Networking Appointment

If you're the one who wants to set up the networking appointment, how you send the request matters.

Here's how many requests look:

JoDee, I would love for you to meet with Sara. She was our summer intern and is looking for a full-time position. I have copied her here and know you will enjoy meeting each other.

Sara – JoDee is a rockstar in HR and she can totally assist you.

OR

JoDee, you have been highly recommended to me as a person I should know. Are you available for coffee next week?

Here's what I'm thinking when I get these messages.

I am flattered to hear this, but what is it you really want? I can likely better serve you by connecting you with a specific person, resource, etc. Chances are, in a week, I might be out of town two days, delivering training one day, and already have a full range of appointments scheduled on the other days. I rarely accept appointments on Fridays because that is the day I play catchup on my projects.

These are our tips for successful networking requests.

Be specific about what you are looking for and why you are reaching out to them in particular. Many people who reach out to me for assistance in finding a new position would be better served if instead of simply asking to meet with me they would say something like, "Hi, I'm reaching out to you for ideas for finding a new role in accounting. My friend, Kim, is a big fan of yours, and she highly recommended you and Purple Ink." In this case, I would immediately connect them with our recruiting and career coaching team, who know the details of our open positions, the best career sites, some jobs open in the market, tips on crafting their resume and LinkedIn profile, etc. I've gotten a bit out of the market on these tips, and my team is much more helpful than I am.

> Tell people why you want to make the connection, what you want from it, and how long it will take.

Be respectful of everyone's time – the time of the person you are reaching out to and your own time.

Consider how much time you really need. Does it need to be in person, or would a quick phone or video call (with no travel time involved) be enough? Don't get too tied to 30 or 60 minutes either. Be more specific about how much time you need and consider asking for a shorter amount of time, like 20, 25, or 45 minutes, instead.

In a nutshell, tell people why you want to make the connection, what you want from it, and how long it will take, and they are more likely to agree to meet with you. At least, I am!

What To Do Next

Once you have met someone new, you have the option to decide what happens next and how you will respond.

I generally connect with everyone I meet on LinkedIn. It is an easy way to stay connected without too much obligation for either of us. I might also link them to Purple Ink's email newsletter.

I ask myself a couple questions to decide if we should connect in another way.

1. Are there any upcoming events we will both be attending? This is an easy way to fit them into my schedule – instead of a

separate meeting, I can join them at a table or chat with them during the cocktail hour.

2. Am I interested in learning more about them or from them?
3. Do I want to connect them with someone else on my team or in my network?
4. Is this a favor for someone who is or might be a strong connection for future referrals or client work?

If I feel that there is no spark, I am not able to assist this person, and they are not a fit for my network, then no follow up is necessary. If I want or expect more from a relationship, I go beyond just connecting on LinkedIn; I add them to my contacts list in Outlook and on my phone. If you are on my contacts list, you are part of my most trusted and respected group.

Great Questions Lead to Great Connections

I have learned not to be afraid to ask questions. I used to think it might show my vulnerabilities or make me look like I did not know enough. Now I understand that asking questions promotes more discussion and shows an interest in others. As they say, people like to talk about themselves.

As Vern Schellenger (CEO of Contacts Count) likes to say, ask stop-and-think questions. People can be like icebergs. Our initial questions help us learn what is above the water for all to see. When we ask stop-and-think questions, we begin to see more of what is below the waterline. This helps us deepen our relationships.

I've also heard the expression "doorknobs" to describe opportunities within a conversation that make people open up more to show different parts of themselves.

The truth is that some people will accept the invitation to provide more detail and some will not. As a JoyPowered® networker, it's your job to give them the opportunity to do so.

It may be as simple as asking someone, "How did you get into your line of work?" or "What do you like the most about your work?" You may share something about your own professional experiences and then organically see opportunities to empathize with one another, offer resources to help each other or even see possible collaborations. You won't know if you don't ask these "doorknob" and "stop-and-think" questions.

Vern describes it as listening for "the Give." I love this terminology. Rather than simply listening for the moment when you can talk about yourself, also listen for what you can give the other person that they would value. This "Give" does not need to be complicated. It might be simply listening actively and empathetically, sharing learnings you've had, or giving an introduction to someone who could be of value to them.

These gives are the magic of JoyPowered® networking. If you focus on them rather than looking to take stage and tell, you will reap the true benefits of connection that come from authentic networking.

Key Takeaways

1. **Find doorknobs that open conversation to new areas of discovery where true connection can happen**. They require active, empathic listening.

2. **Seek ways to give**. Rather than waiting for your turn, be on the lookout for ways to add value to the connection. You will reap the intrinsic benefits from JoyPowered® networking. By "paying it forward" you will assuredly reap benefits down the road.

3. **Do not ignore magic when you feel it**. Be willing to deepen relationships that you sense will become JoyPowered®. This may require that you make shifts in your priorities, but being open to that shift is the way meaningful networks are formed.

8

DON'T BE AFRAID TO BE
AN EXPERT

I am a networking pro, always open to meeting others to learn and share. Here is one of my favorite networking stories about finding my daughter a date:

My sister and I were flying from Indianapolis to Fort Myers with my mother's dog. The plane was pretty full. I was in the middle of our row, my sister was by the window, and the dog went back and forth between our laps. Eventually, the handsome young man next to me (in the aisle seat) took off his headphones and engaged with us about the dog. One thing led to another, and I began talking about my oldest daughter. I eventually shared a photo of her and suggested that they may want to meet. With her permission, I shared her number, and the two of them ended up going on a few dates.

It was a fun networking experience that evolved organically. I never imagined our original discussion about the dog would lead to this, but the more we opened up with one another, the more possibilities I saw for a connection. While my daughter and the cute guy on the plane did not end up together, I know that we were all better for having listened, learned, and been receptive to possibilities.

(You may think of me as the annoying person next to you on the plane, but I did wait for him to engage, albeit with the help of the dog.)

> Being able to articulate your expertise is an important part of JoyPowered® networking.

I enjoy meeting new people, so networking isn't work for me. But doing it well has taken years of fine-tuning how I listen, respond, and invite conversation that brings depth and value to all involved. I now believe I am an expert at this.

Being able to articulate your expertise is an important part of JoyPowered® networking.

Don't Be Bashful

While we said in Chapter 7 that you should help others take stage and share first, you must also be unafraid to share yourself when the time is right. Whatever your expertise is, do not be bashful about sharing it. Not everyone gets to see you in action, but most of us would like to know what others do well so that we can turn to them if we need them or refer them if there is an occasion for it.

Great networking includes communicating your own story. This does not have to be a full re-sume, but it should be a concise way of telling the other person what you do and why they may

> The biggest problem most people face in showcasing their expertise is not being able to do so concisely.

want to know you. This is not bragging, but it should not be pompous or exaggerated.

I have listened to many people share their stories well and many share them poorly. The biggest problem most people face in showcasing their expertise is not being able to do so concisely. If you are a fairly proficient networker, model it for others. Sometimes people don't know how to tightly communicate their story, so they need to see it in action.

Let me give you an example of a poor answer to "tell me what you do."

I met a woman once on a video networking call and after some small talk, asked her to tell me about her work. It turned out that she was looking for a job and she had a job interview the next day. I listened to her complain about all her past jobs and the reasons they didn't work for **18 minutes.**

When she finally paused, there was a long silence. She didn't ask me a question or even appear to know how to shift to me, so I finally said politely that I appreciated what she had shared, had taken notes on what she was looking for, and didn't have anyone I could connect her to at that time. I then thought to myself, "How can I be of help to her?"

I determined that this was NOT a networking opportunity, but rather a coaching opportunity. The best thing I could do was offer her some advice on handling the job interview she had the next day, so I said that she may want to tighten things up and share the learnings she had from her past jobs as a way to sound more positive and professional. I knew it was a bold move, but I also knew the relationship was probably a one-time connection. While I did not want to be seen as rude, I genuinely thought this advice was the best thing I could offer her.

Being an Expert Networker Carries Responsibilities

I have a very special opportunity in my life right now to be leading a national network of consultants in the people space. In this role, I get to tap all of my networking and relationship-building skills regularly. I meet new people, connect people to one another, and aim to facilitate opportunities for those within my network on a daily basis. I am not only doing work I love, but I'm getting lots of practice on the skills needed to make and preserve vital connections.

Humbly and gratefully, I say that I am becoming an expert in the field of networking. When I meet a new person or reconnect with an existing relationship, I not only get to practice, but I get to share my expertise with them. I do not have to tell someone I'm a professional networker. Rather, I show them by the way I network with them.

How I Conduct a Networking Call

When I meet a new person who may have an interest in joining our network, oftentimes via video call, I have a game plan.

I start out by seeking to learn about them. While I've done my homework to know the basics, I want them to share freely as much as they want. I take notes and ask questions so that they know I'm listening and retaining what they say. They feel valued and heard. I ask stop-and-think questions.

Then, when the time is right (a pause or a clear connection to my work), I tell them some version of this 90-second story:

(**Note:** I aim for about 90 seconds because I think 30 seconds can be too short, but much more than 90 can feel like I am telling a full story before I even know if my listener is interested in it.)

I'm a marketer by trade. Two years ago, my good friend JoDee Curtis invited me to join her on a new venture. JoDee is the successful owner of Purple Ink, an established HR consultancy in Central Indiana. She's a rock star, so when she invited me to partner with her to grow a national network of consultants in the broader people space, I was thrilled. Not only did I get to work with someone I admire deeply, but I also got to tap into all of my natural talents – communication, connection, and influence – while meeting inspiring people all over the country.

So, here we are, with about 75 professionals in our network all around the country. We are all invested in helping one another grow our businesses by learning together, partnering, networking, and referring one another. It's magical! Every day I get to meet and learn from coaches, trainers, speakers, HR folks, and other "people professionals" who are consulting with leaders about their workforce issues. I feel like I'm learning all about the challenges that are rampant in the workplace and the solutions presenting themselves.

Then I listen for any questions they have and begin a conversation about how they network to grow their business. Ultimately, I agree to never forget them and to stay connected. If there is reason for us to do business, I remain open to that idea.

Modeling for Others

When I meet with or lead professionals within our network, I aim to always model networking expertise so that they can learn how to do it for themselves. It is dynamic and exciting. I love it. It fuels me. I see the benefits of my work, so when I share my expertise in a new moment, I am confident that I am sharing well and authentically.

What Are You an Expert At?

While I may regard myself as a networking pro, I know that is NOT how to start a conversation – even if that's what I want others to see in me. Rather, I give them stories about connections and approaches that have served me and others within my network well, thus positioning myself as an expert in the field of networking. This becomes one factor in their decision about whether they see value in joining our network. While there will be other factors in their decision, they would not consider it if they didn't have confidence in my ability to lead the network effectively.

Even if they decide not to join our network, I have confidence that they see me as an expert in the field and will remember that in the future. I've done this not simply by saying, "I'm an expert," but by sharing stories about successfully connecting or helping people grow their professional circles and businesses. I also always hope that I've modeled how to be an expert without being a jerk and that they learn something when they move on in their networking journey.

> Nobody believes you're an expert just because you say you are.

In other words, don't lead with, "I'm an expert at...." Rather, give a concise description of the work you do, and then augment it with great stories that illustrate your expertise.

Don't Do This

At one networking meeting, when I asked a guy how he was doing, he responded, "I'm a winner. I've been winning all day today." This is NOT how you showcase your expertise. Nobody believes you're an expert just because you say you are. Again, tell them what you do, and then if you have the chance, use stories to help them come to their own conclusion about your expertise.

Key Takeaways

- **Know what you want people to know about you** and practice articulating it concisely and with relevant and engaging stories.
- **Do not be afraid to be an expert.** People want to know and affiliate with people who are good at their work.
- **Be prepared with good stories** that highlight your expertise. Share them as engaging and illustrative examples.

9

ADD VALUE

JoyPowered® networking is not one-sided. All parties derive value from the connection. If our only goal is to meet and build relationships with others to promote ourselves, it will likely lead to short-term relationships and possibly resentment. The best relationships are those that grow, develop, and are nurtured by all parties. The easiest – and the most fun – way to achieve our best networking is to constantly add value for others and to have them do the same for us. Whether we are learning, being mentored, advising, being referred, or even making a friend, there are many ways to add value to (and receive value from) networking.

> If our only goal is to meet and build relationships with others to promote ourselves, it will likely lead to short-term relationships and possibly resentment.

Here's an example of a mutually valuable networking opportunity:

About six years ago I was asked to join, and later elected, to the board of a $2 billion credit union. Although it was not a paid position, there were some nice benefits and significant networking opportunities. When I started, I knew one person on the board from the HR community. Now, I have two significant client connections, a new attorney, multiple friends, and a new group of professional connections. This board position has added significantly to my network, and I have learned immensely from the people and the experience. My new connections benefited, too. When they needed help with HR, they had someone to call that they already trusted. The attorney gained a new client (me). My friends and connections from the board can go to me for advice, just as I can go to them. Everybody wins!

The beauty of focusing on the value you can *give* is that when you do this, you are less likely to walk away disappointed because you didn't get what you came for. It also takes some of the pressure off you to get something from the other person. If we spend our energy listening and considering how we can give something to the other person, we stop thinking about what we are going to ask them for.

For those who are not comfortable with networking, it can be stressful to walk up to people and introduce yourself, join an already ongoing conversation, and focus on how you want to start the conversation. By not worrying as much about what you are going to ask the other person for, you have the potential opportunity to give them something (a connection, an attentive ear, etc.), but not the pressure that you *must* deliver something of value. If you don't have something to give, you can simply say, "I don't currently have any advice or connections I can make for you."

For us, it's been refreshing to reframe how we regard the purpose of first meetings. This may not always be the case, but it can be quite liberating.

Value Comes in Many Shapes and Sizes

When people think of the word "value," they often think of financial value first. That is not the kind of value we focus on in JoyPowered® networking. Rather, we regard value like a gift. Some of the best gifts do not cost a lot of money or take a lot of time to make. They are thoughtful remembrances, time spent together, or shared experiences.

Think of giving value to a new connection in the same way. Rather than pondering how you can help them close a deal or find a job, listen to them and respond in a thoughtful way. Perhaps it is an empathetic ear, a constructive idea for their work, or a person they should meet. We do not have to have our gift in hand before we meet a new person. We can give value to a new connection simply by being a good listener.

I know of several new connections I've made through LinkedIn where by the end of our meeting, I've offered them a fresh idea for how to market their business or suggested an introduction to someone who may help them solve a business problem they are having. I have done this by listening empathetically.

> We can give value to a new connection simply by being a good listener.

We all have something of value to share with a new connection. Do not minimize your value because you can't put cash in another person's pocket!

Sometimes it Takes Time to Realize the Value

Just like fine wine and flowers, sometimes the sweetness of something takes time. Most of the time, we do not gain immediate value from a single meeting. Rather, that value grows over time or even appears down the road.

I can think of many relationships that started out one way and later became much more, like the parent of my child's friend who became a business referral and invited me to serve on the board he chaired. This does not happen if we are impatient or greedy. It unfolds when we are selfless in how we give value to others and earn their trust.

Key Takeaways

- Seek first to give, and getting will follow.
- We all have value to give to others, even if it is simply listening.
- Value can be given and received over time.

10

LET'S GET PRACTICAL

Now that you understand how true JoyPower can come from net-working, we would like to share some practical tips for how to network well.

Virtual Networking

While we both enjoy a luncheon or after-work networking event where we get to meet new people in person, we have also come to treasure meeting people virtually. This can happen through social media, shared webinar experiences, introductions, and more. The key is to have a strategy to use these opportunities to grow your network in a meaning-ful and fruitful way.

Be Prepared

Let's start with preparing for the great big world of possibilities out there. Our colleague Peggy Hogan, VP of Talent Services at Purple Ink, has some helpful advice about how to prepare yourself to expand your network.

1. Start with who you know. You may already know your next boss or a person who can introduce you to someone you need to know.

2. Everyone you meet is an opportunity to connect. Do not write anyone off or prejudge them. Listen to learn.

3. Be strategic about forming new connections. Ask yourself, "Who do I want or need to know, and why?"

4. Facilitate introductions. Giving introductions is a great way to form stronger relationships.

5. Have a well-practiced (but not too robotic) self-introduction that you can say in approximately 30 seconds. This is a concise answer to, "Tell me about yourself," that you can expound upon later if the conversation continues.

When given an opportunity to share more about yourself (for instance, in a situation that may lead to a job), Peggy suggests you consider the art of sharing and how to incorporate the past, present, and future in your story.

> Do not write anyone off or prejudge them.

PRESENT: Lead with the present. Wow with the now. What is it that you do well and want them to know first about you?

PAST: Give a few highlights about your past. What are the most notable parts of your past that you think they should know?

FUTURE: Now, connect the dots and highlight how you see the future! Describe how what you have done in your past has prepared you for what you want next.

LinkedIn

LinkedIn is the best way to build a virtual professional network. It's a platform designed specifically for business connections and when used properly can help educate, connect, and promote each of us.

We have both formed connections through LinkedIn that have become substantive. Our focus is on building a quality network, not just increasing the quantity of our connections.

To improve your LinkedIn networking, start with yourself. Here are some tactics Peggy Hogan recommends to look your best on LinkedIn:

1. Keep your profile up to date. Include the relevant work you have done that defines you best.
2. Update your headline. You have 220 characters to describe yourself. Use them all. They provide searchable information so others can find you.
3. Let people know if you are available to work or consult. Use posts to showcase your talents and thought leadership and not to tell people you are looking for work. Reach out to individuals to share what you are looking for.
4. Use the advanced search function to research companies you're interested in and follow them so you know what they are up to. This is a great way to connect with companies you may want to work for or with, but also a way to stay abreast of industry trends and knowledge.

   Share your own content. You have something to say.

5. Connect with people who attend the same virtual events as you. Reach out to them afterward and use the shared experience as a basis for connecting.
6. Build your first-degree network. Search for people you want to connect with. You can search by geography, companies, or titles.
7. Ask trusted connections for introductions to their network. If there's someone you want to know, find connections you have in common and ask. The worst thing that can happen is they say no.
8. Engage. People enjoy being heard and supported. Click the bell icon on profiles to be notified when they post. Engage with their content. You will learn about them and the topics that interest them and form better relationships with them.
9. Join professional groups. This is a great way to gain industry knowledge.

10. If you are job searching, research people you'll interview with or possible future bosses.

11. Share your own content. You have something to say. People are drawn to others' thoughts more than they are their profile pictures or positions. If you need help to develop your voice, reach out to a LinkedIn coach.

Key Takeaways

- **Create an accurate virtual representation of yourself.** Be thorough, yet concise, to attract meaningful and appropriate connections.

- **Engage with others.** Virtual networking requires outreach. Don't expect people to come to you. Be proactive and participate to develop relationships that matter.

- **Have a solid elevator pitch AND a more thorough story to tell.** These take practice to nail down. Keep working at them both.

11

JOYPOWERED® NETWORKING FOR JOB SEEKERS

Peggy Hogan, VP of Talent Services at Purple Ink, is a great networker and coach for people looking for their next role. She gave us great ideas to share with you.

60-70% of people get their jobs through their network.

Networking Can Lead to Your Next Job

60-70% of people get their jobs through their network. Oftentimes, this is how you find the hidden jobs that are not advertised or posted. Regardless of how easily networking comes to you, it is THE most important part of a successful job search. If you are already doing it, you are halfway there. If not, here are some tips to start the process.

Make a list of:

- Former colleagues
- Friends and neighbors who work at companies you're interested in
- Former classmates
- Former professors
- Friends of friends

- Anyone you meet at a party, church, sports organization, etc.

Start connecting with all those individuals on LinkedIn or via email. One by one, ask if they are available to grab a cup of coffee or meet to chat. Tell them you are seeking a new position and want their advice. At the end of the conversation, ask if they can think of any companies or organizations that you should check out or anyone you should meet. Your goal is networking, and you can tell them that directly. Try to meet at least one or two people a week.

Sample Messages

If you need to reach out to people regarding a specific job through email or LinkedIn, below are a few sample messages:

Sample 1:

Hi [NAME],

I wanted to let you know that I submitted my application for the [JOB TITLE] role at [COMPANY]. I know they may be inundated with resumes and sometimes a word from an internal person can help a candidate stand out. Would you be willing to facilitate an introduction to the hiring manager?

I appreciate any help you can provide!

Sample 2:

Hi [NAME],

I hope all is well with you! I am looking for a new career opportunity and see that you are connected to [NAME] who works at [COMPANY]. I have applied to the [JOB TITLE] role at [COMPANY]. I am sure they have a lot of applicants and I wondered if you would be so kind as to pass my name and resume along to [NAME] to ask that my information gets a solid review?

I appreciate any help you can provide!

Expanding Your Network

Many people refer to the groups they participate in as "circles." For this reason, when we are inviting people to figure out who they can network with, we ask them to imagine networking "circles."

Here are some of the circles we suggest to consider as part of your own personal network. Create a diagram like the one below, with circles for each group you participate in. In each circle, list the people in that group that you could network with or reach out to for introductions.

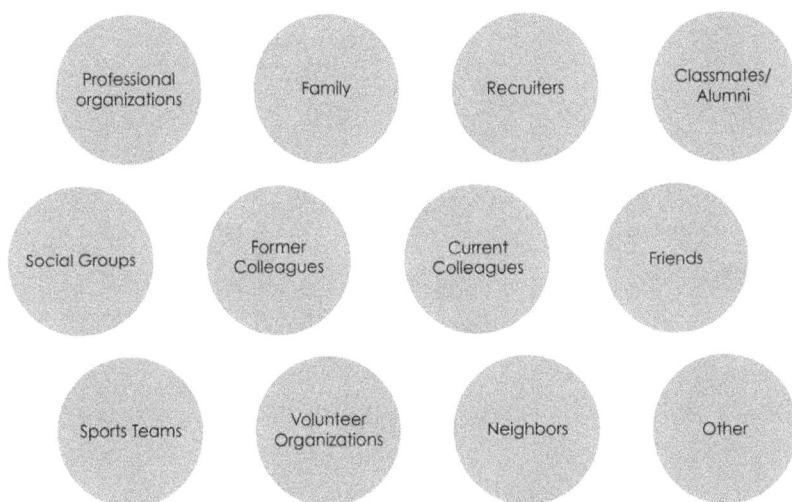

Professional organizations · Family · Recruiters · Classmates/Alumni

Social Groups · Former Colleagues · Current Colleagues · Friends

Sports Teams · Volunteer Organizations · Neighbors · Other

Some circles may be bigger or a more significant part of your network than others. Professional organizations, as an example, have played a major role in my networking, while others may not have a robust professional organization to tap into.

There could be different purposes for different circles, as well. Your professional organization network may be helpful if you are looking for a new role or a good source of continuing education hours. You might think of your friends circle for socializing and entertainment, but they could also provide referrals to you or connect you with people who might be a good fit to join your team. Former colleagues could serve as mentors, references, and referrals.

Here is another graphic to help you identify how to expand your network. Start with a company that appeals to you (or the one you currently work for), and expand from there. Who is their competition? Who are their customers? Suppliers? These additional people can broaden your network for possible work, customers, and current trends.

The more specific you are in your request, the easier it is for them to accomplish the task.

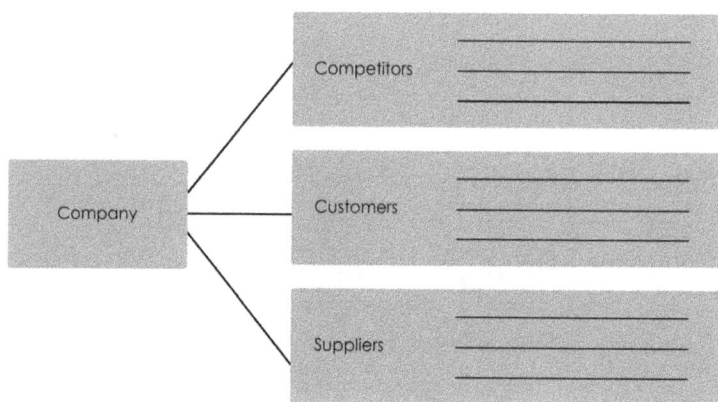

In a nutshell, reach out to people. Most people are happy to help with introductions or ideas. The more specific you are in your request, the easier it is for them to accomplish the task. I have had people ask me for a reference and include a draft of the reference for me. For example:

Hi JoDee,

I hope you're doing well!

I'm applying for a new position and was hoping you might provide a reference for me. To make it easier, I've included some wording you might use below, but please don't feel any pressure to use it if you disagree or would rather write your own. I appreciate your help!

I worked with Rob in the '80s, and we were both auditors. I enjoyed working on Rob's team because he was very organized, did not procrastinate, and took the time to share great feedback with me on a regular basis.

Another idea is to send an email or LinkedIn message connecting two people you know; it might look like this:

Rob, I'd like to introduce you to Christine. She is a speaker on the topic of JoyPowered® Networking, and I remember you telling me this weekend that you were looking for someone to assist you with becoming more confident and selective when networking. Regardless of how it goes, I think you both will enjoy meeting each other and sharing your love of travel.

When you are looking for a job, having a strong network is important. Don't wait to form one until the moment you need or want a new job. Consider all of these ongoing strategies for forming a professional network of others whom you can turn to if and when the time comes to leverage those relationships in your job search.

Key Takeaways

- **Start with the people you know.** You will be surprised how many people in your current network can introduce you to other great connections.
- **Find a message that works and send it to everyone.** Fine-tune the email or LinkedIn language that you are comfortable with and start sending it out to set up meetings.
- **Tap the pros for more information on networking during a job search.** There are many recruiters out there with advice for the immediate job market. Keep current.

WRAP UP: GO FORTH WITH JOYPOWERED® NETWORKING

In this book, we wanted to capture all the joy and benefits we derive from networking and share our tips and strategies with you. We believe wholeheartedly that there are a lot of great people to meet and know and that JoyPowered® networking is the way to find them and form meaningful, reciprocal relationships.

We hope this book inspires you and teaches you how to take the theory of networking and put it into practice.

As leaders in this space, we are also participants in the vast professional network of people seeking to meet other people. Let your first JoyPowered® networking move be connecting with us. Find us on LinkedIn! You can search for our names, or you'll find direct links in Appendix C.

Consider us both part of your professional network.

APPENDIX A: PERSONAL NOTES ON *JOYPOWERED® NETWORKING*

I have gained the following insights from reading *JoyPowered® Networking*.

Chapter 1: Networker, Know Yourself

Insight 1

_____

_____

_____

Insight 2

_____

_____

_____

Chapter 2: Be Strategic

Insight 1

_____

_____

_____

Insight 2

_____

_____

_____

Chapter 3: Stop Waiting for JoyPowered® Networking to Happen

Insight 1

_____

_____

_____

Insight 2

_____

_____

_____

Chapter 4: Know When to Hold and When to Fold

Insight 1

_____

_____

_____

Insight 2

_____

_____

_____

Chapter 5: Timing and Trust

Insight 1

_____
_____
_____

Insight 2

_____
_____
_____

Chapter 6: JoyPowered® Networking Requires Practice

Insight 1

_____
_____
_____

Insight 2

_____
_____
_____

Chapter 7: Follow the Sparks

Insight 1

_____
_____

Insight 2

_____

_____

_____

Chapter 8: Don't Be Afraid to Be an Expert

Insight 1

_____

_____

_____

Insight 2

_____

_____

_____

Chapter 9: Add Value

Insight 1

_____

_____

_____

Insight 2

_____

_____

_____

Chapter 10: Let's Get Practical

Insight 1

_____

_____

_____

Insight 2

_____

_____

_____

Chapter 11: JoyPowered® Networking for Job Seekers

Insight 1

_____

_____

_____

Insight 2

_____

_____

_____

APPENDIX B: JOYPOWERED®
NETWORKING ACTION PLAN

I will initiate the following actions to inspire JoyPowered® networking:

Immediately:

1. _____
2. _____
3. _____
4. _____

In One Month:

1. _____
2. _____
3. _____
4. _____

In Three Months:

1. _____
2. _____
3. _____
4. _____

In Six Months:

1. _____
2. _____
3. _____
4. _____

In One Year:

1. _____
2. _____
3. _____
4. _____

APPENDIX C:
ADDITIONAL RESOURCES

Chapter 1: Networker, Know Yourself

1. The Purple Ink blog: "Name, Claim, and Aim Your Strengths" https://purpleinkllc.com/2015/06/16/name-claim-and-aim-your-strengths/
2. The JoyPowered® Workspace Podcast: "Utilizing the Clifton StrengthsFinder Assessment" https://getjoypowered.com/show-notes-episode-6-utilizing-the-clifton-strengthsfinder-assessment/
3. CliftonStrengths® Themes Quick Reference Card https://www.gallup.com/workplace/245090/cliftonstrengths-themes-quick-reference-card.aspx

Chapter 2: Be Strategic

1. The Purple Ink blog: "3 Tips on How to Expand Your Professional Network" https://purpleinkllc.com/2018/09/26/3-tips-on-how-to-expand-your-professional-network/
2. The JoyPowered® Workspace Podcast: "SHRM Credit: Networking" https://getjoypowered.com/show-notes-episode-50-shrm-credit-networking/

Chapter 3: Stop Waiting for JoyPowered® Networking to Happen

1. The Purple Ink blog: "Make Time to Volunteer" https://purplein-kllc.com/2017/12/13/make-time-to-volunteer/
2. The JoyPowered® Workspace Podcast: "Propel Your Career through Volunteer Leadership" https://getjoypowered.com/show-notes-ep-isode-44-propel-your-career-through-volunteer-leadership/

Chapter 4: Know When to Hold and When to Fold

1. The Purple Ink blog: "How to Remove the Fear of Feedback" https://purpleinkllc.com/2019/03/27/how-to-remove-the-fear-of-feedback/
2. The Purple Ink blog: "Some Dos and Don'ts of HR Friendships" https://purpleinkllc.com/2016/05/25/some-dos-and-donts-of-hr-friendship/
3. The JoyPowered® Workspace Podcast: "How to Have Difficult Conversations at Work (SHRM Credit)" https://joypowered.podbean.com/e/how-to-have-difficult-conversations-at-work-shrm-credit/

Chapter 5: Timing and Trust

1. The Purple Ink blog: "How Trusted Is Your Coach?" https://pur-pleinkllc.com/2017/09/20/how-trusted-is-your-coach/
2. The Purple Ink blog: "Virtue in the Workplace: Trustworthiness" https://purpleinkllc.com/2019/01/28/virtue-in-the-workplace-trustworthiness/

Chapter 6: Joypowered® Networking Requires Practice

1. *Strategic Connections: The New Face of Networking in a Collaborative World* https://www.amazon.com/ Strategic-Connections-Networking-Collaborative-World/ dp/0814434967
2. Tom Kuegler's LinkedIn Sprint https://www.tomkuegler.com/ linkedin-sprint
3. Jen Slagle's website (she sometimes offers classes about LinkedIn) https://jenslagle.com/
4. JAKAPA https://jakapa.com/

Chapter 7: Follow the Sparks

1. The Purple ink blog: "Enhancing Your Communication Image" https://purpleinkllc.com/2021/06/02/ enhancing-your-communication-image/
2. The JoyPowered® Workspace Podcast: "SHRM Credit: Enhancing Your Business Communications" https://joypowered.podbean. com/e/shrm-credit-enhancing-your-business-communications/

Chapter 8: Don't Be Afraid to Be an Expert

1. The Purple Ink blog: "So You Want to Honor Your True Potential...Now What?" https://purpleinkllc.com/2022/05/04/ so-you-want-to-honor-your-true-potential-now-what/
2. The Purple Ink blog: "How to Answer the Most Dreaded Interview Questions: Tell Me About Yourself" https://purpleinkllc.com/2020/11/18/how-to-answer-the-most-dreaded-interview-questions-tell-me-about-yourself/
3. The Purple Ink blog: "Tell a Story, Get the Job: Tips for

Using Storytelling to Ace the Interview" https://purpleinkllc. com/2019/08/07/tell-a-story-get-the-job-tips-for-using-storytelling-to-ace-the-interview/

Chapter 9: Add Value

1. The JoyPowered® Workspace Podcast: "Building a Tribe" https://joypowered.podbean.com/e/building-a-tribe/The JoyPowered® Workspace Podcast: "Powering Up the People Profession (Sponsored Episode)" https://joypowered.podbean. com/e/powering-up-the-people-profession-sponsored-episode/
2. The Powered by Purple Ink blog: "5 Keys to Becoming a Great Giver (and Recipient) of Referrals" https://poweredbypurpleink. com/5-keys-to-becoming-a-great-giver-and-recipient-of-referrals/
3. The Powered by Purple Ink blog: "6 Steps to Making a Great Professional Introduction" https://poweredbypurpleink.com/6-steps-to-making-a-great-professional-introduction/

Chapter 10: Let's Get Practical

1. The Purple Ink blog: "Networking = Asking for Introductions" https://purpleinkllc.com/2015/10/16/ networking-asking-for-introductions/
2. The Powered by Purple Ink blog: "Using LinkedIn to Build a Valuable Personal Professional Network" https://poweredbypurpleink.com/ using-linkedin-to-build-a-valuable-personal-professional-network/

Chapter 11: JoyPowered® Networking for Job Seekers

1. The Purple Ink blog: "6 Steps to Start a Successful Job Search" https://purpleinkllc.com/2015/08/06/6-steps-to-start-a-successful-job-search/

2. The JoyPowered® Workspace Podcast, "SHRM Credit: How to Start a Job Search and Negotiate Salary" https://getjoypowered.com/show-notes-episode-8-shrm-credit-how-to-start-a-job-search-and-negotiate-salary/

3. Frank Agin (he facilitates the Networking Hub, a monthly Zoom gather of coaches and consultants) https://www.frankagin.com/

4. HRHotSeat https://www.hrhotseat.com/

Wrap Up: Go Forth Networking with JoyPower

1. Christine's LinkedIn https://www.linkedin.com/in/christine-burrows-pbpi/

2. JoDee's LinkedIn https://www.linkedin.com/in/jodee-curtis-csp-shrm-scp-cpa-064a611/

APPENDIX D: REFERENCES

1. Curtis, JoDee, *JoyPowered: Intentionally Creating an Inspired Workspac.e* BookBaby, 2016.
2. Curtis, JoDee and McGonigal, Denise, *The JoyPowered Family.* BookBaby, 2018.
3. Brothers, Erin et al., *The JoyPowered Team.* BookBaby, 2019.
4. Curtis, JoDee et al., *The JoyPowered Organization.* BookBaby, 2021.
5. "CliftonStrengths." *Gallup Store*, store.gallup.com/c/en-us/ CliftonStrengths. Accessed 31 May 2023.
6. "The Benefits of Networking: 14 Reasons to Start Your Network." *Indeed*, 22 July 2022, www.indeed.com/career-advice/ career-development/benefit-of-networking.
7. "CliftonStrengths Quick Reference Card." *Gallup.Com*, 12 Oct. 2020, www.gallup.com/workplace/245090/cliftonstrengths-themes-quick-reference-card.aspx.
8. "What Do I Know about Networking?" *Contacts Count*, www.contactscount.com/blog/what-do-i-know-about-networking-2. Accessed 9 June 2023.
9. Baber, Anne, et al. *Strategic Connections: The New Face of Networking in a Collaborative World.* AMACOM, 2015.
10. *JAKAPA*, 16 May 2023, jakapa.com/.

REVIEW INQUIRY

Hey, it's JoDee and Christine here.

We hope you've enjoyed the book, finding it both useful and fun. We have a favor to ask you.

Would you consider giving it a rating wherever you bought the book? Online book stores are more likely to promote a book when they feel good about its content, and reader reviews are a great barometer for a book's quality.

So please go to the website of wherever you bought the book, search for our names and the book title, and leave a review. If able, perhaps consider adding a picture of you holding the book. That increases the likelihood your review will be accepted!

Many thanks in advance,
JoDee Curtis and Christine Burrows

WILL YOU SHARE THE LOVE?

Get this book for a friend, associate, or family member!

If you have found this book valuable and know others who would find it useful, consider buying them a copy as a gift. Special bulk discounts are available if you would like your whole team or organization to benefit from reading this. Just contact networking@getjoypowered.com.

WOULD YOU LIKE JODEE AND CHRISTINE TO SPEAK TO YOUR ORGANIZATION?

Book Jodee and Christine Now!

JoDee and Christine accept a limited number of speaking, coaching, and training engagements each year. To learn how you can bring their message to your organization, email networking@getjoypowered.com or visit getjoypowered.com.

OTHER BOOKS IN THE JOYPOWERED® SERIES

ABOUT THE AUTHORS

Jodee Curtis, CSP, SHRM-SCP, CPA
JoDee is the Founder of Purple Ink and Powered by Purple Ink. She has a passion for helping organizations and individuals discover their talents, do more of what they do well, and find joy in their work.

JoDee has a unique combination of experience as a CPA, CFO, and VP of HR. She has 30+ years of experience in HR and is especially passionate about training and speaking to inspire others. She is the creator of the JoyPowered® philosophy, an author of each book in the JoyPowered® series, and co-host of the JoyPowered® Workspace Podcast.

Christine Burrows, Ed.M
Christine is the Vice President of Strategy and Operations for Purple Ink. Meeting and connecting new people is in her DNA.

Christine spent 10+ years working in media productions, developing content for teachers to use in their classrooms, then ran her own content marketing business, working with various clients to build and sustain websites that attract and retain targeted clients.

JoDee and Christine can be reached at: purpleinkllc.com

www.ingramcontent.com/pod-product-compliance
Lightning Source LLC
Chambersburg PA
CBHW071435210326
41597CB00020B/3799